Festivals *of the* World

SPAIN

TIMES EDITIONS

Written by
SUSAN MCKAY

Edited by
AUDREY LIM

Designed by
HASNAH MOHD ESA

Picture research by
SUSAN JANE MANUEL

© **TIMES EDITIONS PTE LTD 1999**
Originated and designed by
Times Books International
an imprint of Times Editions Pte Ltd
Times Center, 1 New Industrial Road
Singapore 536196
Tel: 2848844
Fax: 2854871
E-mail: te@corp.tpl.com.sg
Online Bookstore:
http://www.timesone.com.sg/te

Times Subang
Lot 46, Subang Hi-Tech Industrial Park
Batu Tiga 40000 Shah Alam
Selangor Darul Ehsan Malaysia
Fax & Tel: (603) 7363517
E-mail: cchong@tpg.com.my

Printed in Singapore

ISBN 981 204 934 7

CONTENTS

It's Festival Time . . .

In Spain, the word for "festival" is *fiesta* [fee-AYS-tah]. Many Spanish fiestas are known throughout the world, and people travel hundreds, even thousands, of miles to celebrate them. Part of the fun is joining in the singing, dancing, and general merrymaking that surround nearly all festivals in Spain. So, come along and run with the bulls, dress up in fancy costumes, or learn the *flamenco*. It's festival time in Spain . . .

WHERE'S SPAIN?

Spain is located at the southwestern tip of Europe. A narrow waterway, called the Strait of Gibraltar, separates Spain from Africa. Its closest African

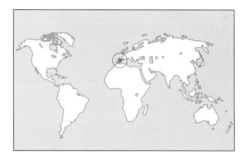

neighbor is Morocco. To the north, its neighbors are Andorra and France and, to the west, Portugal. The Mediterranean Sea lies to the south and east, and mountain ranges are found in the north and south of the country. Spain is the third largest country in Europe. Its capital is Madrid.

Who are the Spaniards?

Spaniards are a very **diverse** people. The 40 million people who live in Spain come from many different backgrounds and speak many different languages. Most Spaniards identify themselves by their native region, instead of by their nationality.

A smiling Spaniard in Asturias wearing a festival outfit.

SPAIN

FRANCE

Bay of Biscay

Golfe du Lion

ANDORRA

ASTURIAS

CANTABRIA

BASQUE COUNTRY

Pamplona •

NAVARRA

Pyrenees

GALICIA

CASTILE-LEÓN

LA RIOJA

• Saragossa

• Barcelona

ARAGÓN

CATALONIA

Segovia •

A T L A N T I C   O C E A N

• MADRID

VALENCIA

Minorca

PORTUGAL

• Toledo

Balearic Islands

Majorca

N

ESTREMADURA

CASTILE-LA MANCHA

Valencia •

Ibiza

• Alcoy

• Alicante

Córdoba •

MURCIA

Seville •

ANDALUSIA

Sistemas Béticos

M E D I T E R R A N E A N   S E A

Gibraltar (Br.)

Strait of Gibraltar

• Ceuta (Spain)

ALGERIA

• Melilla (Spain)

CANARY ISLANDS

MOROCCO

Santa Cruz de Tenerife

An example of Spanish architecture, the Alcazar in Segovia.

WHEN'S THE FIESTA?

There is always plenty to do at our festivals. Turn the page and see!

SPRING

- ✪ **SAINT JOSEPH'S DAY**
- ✪ **LA MAYA**—Men cut down tall trees, strip them of their branches, decorate them with flowers and ribbons, and take them to the village square, where they stand throughout May.
- ✪ **DAY OF THE CROSS**—People set up crosses covered with leaves and flowers on their patios at home. The family sings and dances around the cross to commemorate Christ's crucifixion.
- ✪ **SAN ISIDRO DAY**
- ✪ **QUEEN ISABELLA DAY**—Honors the birth of the Spanish queen who **sponsored** Columbus' voyage to the New World.
- ✪ **ARBOR DAY**
- ✪ **HOLY WEEK**
- ✪ **FERIA DE ABRIL**
- ✪ **MOORS AND CHRISTIANS FESTIVAL**

SUMMER

- **SAN ANTONIO DAY**—Honors the patron saint of animals with a procession, fireworks, and a carnival.
- **SAINT JOHN'S DAY**
- **EL DÍA DE LA ASUNCIÓN**—People nail olive branches and wheat heads to the wall to ensure peace and bread all year.
- **FIESTA DE SAN FERMIN**

AUTUMN

- **COLUMBUS DAY**
- **OUR LADY OF VALME DAY**
- **JEREZ DE LA FRONTERA**—A sherry wine harvest festival to celebrate the blessing of the grapes and the first wine of the season.

WINTER

- **SAINT NICHOLAS DAY**
- **CHRISTMAS**
- **HOLY INNOCENT'S DAY**
- **NEW YEAR'S**—Each family member gets 12 grapes. At the stroke of midnight on December 31st, each person eats one grape for each stroke to bring good luck each month of the coming year.
- **EPIPHANY**
- **SAINT BLAISE'S DAY**—Children eat small loaves of blessed bread to protect them from choking on food.

Do you like my outfit? Come with me to see the floats on Saint Joseph's Day!

SAINT JOSEPH'S DAY

T he feast day of Saint Joseph, patron saint of carpenters and Jesus' earthly father, is celebrated on March 19th each year. In the city of Valencia, the festivities last an entire week. At sunrise on the first morning of the festival, the city wakes up to the explosion of thousands of fireworks signaling the start of the celebration. For the rest of the week, Valencians are treated to a **spectacular** arts exhibition.

Floats for Saint Joseph's Day can take up to a year to make.

The Exaltation

As part of the Saint Joseph's Day festivities, a **Fallas** [FAH-lahss] Queen, or Queen of Floats, is chosen from among the women of Valencia. The Queen is crowned and sworn into office during the ceremony of the Exaltation.

Choosing a Fallas Queen (*above*) and a bonfire of floats (*below*) are part of the celebrations.

Las Fallas

The highlight of Saint Joseph's Day comes when hundreds of fallas (floats) are set on fire. Most floats are designed to poke fun at Spanish politicians, international figures, or famous events that happened in the past year. The floats are displayed and judged, and prizes are awarded. A parade of the floats is held on Saint Joseph's Day Eve. Then, the next night at midnight, all but the winning float are covered with fireworks and set on fire.

How did Las Fallas begin?

Many people believe the tradition of Las Fallas began several hundred years ago in the Middle Ages. According to legend, all the carpenters in Valencia honored Saint Joseph by making bonfires. They burned scraps and sweepings from their workshops. Soon, the fires became a kind of **rivalry**, with each workshop trying to outdo the other. **Effigies** representing rival workshops were built and burned, and old junk was thrown on top of the fire to make the flames higher.

The flower offering

One of the most colorful parts of the festival is the offering of flowers to Our Lady of the Forsaken, Valencia's patron saint. Townspeople dress in their best clothes and travel to the main square carrying bouquets and baskets overflowing with flowers. More than 30 tons of flowers are placed in the square as a tribute to this saint.

These boys are shouldering a heavy responsibility as they carry this enormous bouquet of flowers.

Opposite: Thousands of people come from all over Spain and from other countries to be part of the celebrations on Saint Joseph's Day. This crowd of people shows how popular the festival is!

Think about this

Over the course of history, people have used fire for many important purposes: to cook food, to fight enemies, even to talk to one another. What are the uses of fire today? Even though fire can help people, it is very dangerous when out of control. Can you think of certain events in history when fire proved to be destructive?

HOLY WEEK

oly Week marks the beginning of spring. It usually falls either at the end of March or during April. The week starts with Palm Sunday and ends with Easter. Holy Week traditions in Spain have remained almost the same since the sixteenth century, and nowhere are the Holy Week processions as famous as in the southern city of Seville. Both locals and tourists gather to watch. What are the processions like? Read on to find out!

This girl's solemn expression shows how seriously she takes her role in a Holy Week procession.

Above: The Passion of Christ being presented to the crowd. Have you ever watched a presentation of the Passion?

Tradition takes over

The tradition of Holy Week processions began when the Catholic Church decided to present the Passion of Christ in a way that would be easy for everyone to understand. The best carpenters and craftsmen in the area made huge wooden figures representing the saints. During Holy Week, these figures were paraded through the streets, and the people were deeply moved .

These men are ready to celebrate Holy Week in Seville.

Costaleros

Today, Spaniards celebrate Holy Week with the same traditional fervor. Floats depict different religious scenes with figures dressed in expensive robes and wigs. Men called ***costaleros*** [cos-ta-LAY-ross] carry the floats on their shoulders. A rolled-up sack, or *costal*, placed behind the neck softens the weight. The costaleros are hidden by a long skirt draped around the bottom of the float.

Above: Wearing their hoods, *nazarenos* [nah-zah-RAY-nohss] lead the procession.

Below: There could be up to 40 costaleros under this float, each supporting almost 220 pounds (100 kilograms) on his neck and shoulders.

Left: Young girls moving along with the procession.

Nazarenos

Nazarenos, or penitents, are at the front of Holy Week processions. Penitents are people who are very sorry for something they have done. They dress in long robes with pointed hoods, called *capuchones* [ca-poo-CHOH-nays], and they carry big, heavy crosses. Some nazarenos carry up to four crosses! The capuchones are the same as those worn during the Spanish Inquisition. The Spanish Inquisition questioned people's Christian faith. Some Christians were accused of witchcraft and were even burned at the stake.

Think about this

Each float has a leader who guides and directs the whole group. He makes sure that the costaleros are moving to the same rhythm and tells them when to take a break and when to pick up the float again. He shouts out, "Let's go, my brave ones!" to encourage them.

This boy is putting his lungs to good use.

FERIA DE ABRIL

T wo weeks after Holy Week, Seville is the site of the Feria de Abril, or the April Fair. This fair is considered one of Spain's great spring festivals. Originally, the fair was an annual market for buying and selling animals, crops, and agricultural machinery. Today, although some cattle dealing still goes on, it is just an excuse for Sevillians to celebrate life.

Women enjoying themselves at the fair. Aren't their outfits lovely?

Los Remedios

The fair is set up in Los Remedios, a district of Seville. The fairgrounds stretch for almost a mile. Within the grounds is a **makeshift** city of canvas huts. In between each hut, the streets are covered with golden sand and lined with paper lanterns. Outside the grounds is a huge amusement park complete with rides, games, shows, food stands, and a circus. Children have lots of fun visiting the park with their parents.

Gateway to fun

The entrance to the fairgrounds is a gateway built especially for the fair. The fair begins with the official lighting of hundreds of small lights around the gateway. For the next six days, thousands of people will pass through the gateway from afternoon until dawn. Some people even camp out at the fairgrounds so they won't miss any of the action. There is no shortage of things to do for adults and children.

The horse show

One of the high points of the fair is the horse show. It takes place every day, starting at two o'clock in the afternoon and ending at eight o'clock at night. More than 3,500 horses strut their stuff in an amazing display of color and movement. There are harnessed horses and carriages, and the riders dress in bright, traditional clothes for the occasion. The men wear leather chaps, red cummerbunds, and short jackets; the women wear long, full-skirted dresses with colorful polka dots on them. With such exuberance and excitement, Feria de Abril is one of Spain's most delightful festivals.

Above: Flamenco dances add to the festival's excitement.

This family is enjoying a horseback ride. Have you ever ridden a horse before?

Children eagerly wait for the flamenco dancing to start.

Flamenco

The Feria de Abril is considered the greatest **flamenco** event in Spain. Flamenco is a special kind of Spanish music and dance that is a very important part of Spanish culture. Flamenco is a community event. Everyone takes a turn at singing and dancing, while others encourage them. The music is used as a way to express all kinds of feelings, such as happiness, sadness, love, and hatred. Musicians create the rhythm and mood using guitars and voices.

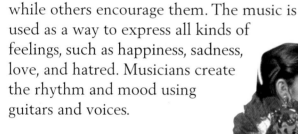

Think about this
In 1997, the Feria de Abril celebrated its 150th anniversary. The fair started in 1847, thanks to the support of Queen Isabel II.

Flamenco has intricate hand movements and takes lots of practice to do well.

FIESTA DE SAN FERMIN

For eight days in July, the city of Pamplona honors San Fermin, its patron saint. This festival was first held in 1591. Ernest Hemingway, an American author who lived in Spain, made it famous by mentioning it in his book, *The Sun Also Rises*. The festival is complete with fireworks, singing, dancing, and fairs. The most spectacular of the festivities, however, is the Running of the Bulls. Each year, thousands of people come from across the world to run with the bulls through the streets of Pamplona.

Above: Souvenirs from the festival.

Below: Running away from the bull.

Viva San Fermin!

Events begin when the president of the festival organizing committee fires a rocket gun from the balcony of City Hall. The huge crowd gathered below the balcony cheers and sings. Champagne bottles are uncorked, and their contents are sprayed on the crowd. People tie red scarves around their necks and shout "Viva San Fermin!" or "Long live San Fermin!" According to legend, Fermin was martyred when Romans tied him to a bull's horns and let the bull drag him to his death. Today, people wait with eager anticipation for the bullfights and the amazing spectacle, the Running of the Bulls, called *Encierro* [en-see-AIR-o].

Above: A bullfight in progress.

Children especially enjoy parades at this festival.

Runners who can't stay ahead of the bulls had better get out of the way!

The Running of the Bulls

The Running of the Bulls has made the Fiesta de San Fermin world famous. It is part of the festivities that celebrate the start of the bullfighting season, and it is held every morning from July 7th to July 14th. It starts at eight o'clock in the morning, when the bulls are led from their pen and turned loose at the end of Santo Domingo street. A rocket is set off the moment the bulls are in the street.

Brave runners gather at the starting line and sing a song to San Fermin. Then, they run in front of the bulls all the way from the pens to the bullring, some 875 yards (800 meters) away! Running with the bulls is very dangerous, and a lot of people get hurt every year. After the event, those who participated in the Encierro gather at taverns to talk about the excitement of the day.

A matador entrancing the crowd with his skills.

The Bullfight

At 6:30 every night, visitors gather at the ring to see a bullfight. This event is filled with color, danger, and daring. For some, bullfighting is a cruel sport, but for others, it is an art. It begins with an entrance parade, in which horsemen dressed in sixteenth century costumes lead **matadors** into the ring. The matadors are followed by *banderilleros* [ban-day-ree-YAY-roz] and mounted picadors, who will help them during the fight. When a white handkerchief is thrown into the ring to signal the entrance of the first bull, the crowds cheer and clap to show their tremendous appreciation for the bulls and matadors.

Acto Final

The final act of the fiesta, a candlelit parade through Pamplona, takes place on July 14th at midnight. The marchers all sing a song, called *Pobre de Mi y Traca*, or *Poor Me*, to mourn the passing of the festival for another year.

A matador in his stunning outfit.

Think about this

The bulls in Pamplona were originally herded and driven to the ring by drovers, similar to cowboys. As time passed, it became a popular event, and people started running in front of the bulls instead of behind them as drovers do.

23

MOORS AND CHRISTIANS FESTIVAL

Until about 500 years ago, Muslims from North Africa, called Moors, ruled southern Spain. They introduced new kinds of medicine, farming, and science to the Christians living there. In 1492 (the same year Columbus landed in the New World), the Christians fought the Muslims in a great battle and drove them out of Spain. Every year, this battle is restaged at the Moors and Christians Festival in Alcoy.

These men will pretend to do battle at the Festival in Alcoy.

A parade and a battle

The festival begins with a grand parade through the streets. Half the marchers are dressed as Moorish soldiers, the other half as Christians. Each year, a boy is chosen to play the warrior, Saint George. The battle is reenacted with more than nine tons of gunpowder and lots of swordplay! After the battle has gone on for a while, the Moors fall back, and the soldiers of Saint George win the day. The crescent flag of the Moors is taken down, and the cross of Saint George is raised. Finally, there is a victory parade complete with fireworks. The soldiers on both sides hug and toast each other, happy to be neighbors once more.

THINGS FOR YOU TO DO

People from all over the world are amazed by the music and dance of Spanish flamenco. Flamenco music is said to be a mixture of two cultures: the culture of Andalusia (in the south of Spain) and the culture of the **Gypsies**.

Who are the Gypsies?

Gypsies, a large ethnic group in Spain, lead a transient life, which means they don't settle down in one place for very long; they are **vagabonds**. Gypsies have a very rich music culture. Music and dancing are part of all their celebrations, so there are hundreds of Gypsy singers, musicians, and dancers. About 300 years ago, the Gypsies invented flamenco. Today, the greatest flamenco stars are Gypsies.

What is flamenco?

Over the years, Gypsies have suffered a lot. Making music and celebrating life was one way to relieve their suffering. Flamenco can be sung, danced, or played. In fact, you can use whatever instruments you like, from a horn, to castanets, to a glass and spoon, to the heels of your shoes. The most famous flamenco performers are singers and guitarists. There are many different flamenco styles, called *palos* [PA-los]. It is very difficult to learn all the different palos, but real flamenco stars master all the styles.

Make castanets

Castanets are often used by dancers during a flamenco performance. They are wooden disks that make a clicking sound when they are tapped together. You can make your own castanets; all you need are two wooden disks with a hole in the middle of each one, some string, paints, and a paintbrush. Paint the disks with bright colors in any pattern you choose. Let the paint dry. Thread string through one disk and make a knot, leaving a loop large enough for your thumb. Then thread the string through the other disk, leaving a loop for your index finger. Be sure the disks are tied together tightly so they don't slip from your fingers. Now, click your castanets in your favorite rhythm!

Things to look for in your library

Faster Than the Bull. Publish-A-Book (series). Lutz Braun (Raintree/Steck-Vaughn, 1993).
Favorite Fairy Tales Told in Spain. Virginia Haviland (Beech Tree Books, 1995).
If I Lived in Spain. Rosanne Knorr (Longstreet Press, 1994).
The Land and Peoples of Spain. Adrian Shubert (Harper Collins Publishers, 1992).
Spain. Neil Champion (Thomson Learning, 1996).
Spain. (Interfilm Journal Films, 1988).
Spain. On the Map (series). Daphne Butler (Raintree/Steck-Vaughn, 1992).
A Visit to Spain. Jackie Gaff (Kingfisher Books, 1994).

MAKE A CARNIVAL MASK

During Carnival, Spaniards dress up in all kinds of elaborate costumes. Giant masks are a common sight, and, depending on the mask, they can be worn either over the head or on top of the head. Follow these instructions and celebrate Carnival the Spanish way.

You will need:
1. Paintbrushes
2. A wax pencil
3. Glue
4. Tape
5. Scissors
6. Stapler
7. Yarn
8. A styrofoam ball cut in half
9. A paint tray
10. Paints
11. A rubber band
12. A balloon
13. Starch
14. A piece of cloth
15. Newspaper

1 Blow up the balloon and close off the end with the rubber band. Dip the entire balloon in starch. Glue newspaper strips onto the balloon and let the glue dry. Remove the rubber band and pull the balloon out of its paper "case."

2 Draw a face on the mask and paint it. Glue on the styrofoam halves and paint them as eyes.

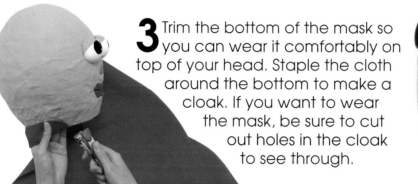

3 Trim the bottom of the mask so you can wear it comfortably on top of your head. Staple the cloth around the bottom to make a cloak. If you want to wear the mask, be sure to cut out holes in the cloak to see through.

4 To make hair for your mask, wind the yarn around your palm until a thick bundle forms. Tie the bundle at one end with a piece of yarn. Cut the other end to remove the yarn from your palm. Tape the mop of "hair" on your mask's head. Now you have your very own Carnival mask.

MAKE CREMA FRITA

C rema Frita means fried custard in Spanish. It is a typical Spanish dessert. Try making this delicious treat but be sure to have an adult help you do the frying!

You will need:
1. A measuring cup
2. 2 cups (480 ml) milk
3. 4 oz. (115 g) butter
4. 4 egg yolks
5. 1 teaspoon vanilla powder or extract
6. A saucepan
7. 2 oz. (60 g) breadcrumbs
8. 2 oz. (60 g) flour
9. 1 egg, beaten
10. Measuring spoons
11. A square cake pan
12. 4 oz. (115 g) sugar
13. A whisk
14. A spatula
15. A sieve
16. Powdered sugar

1 and 2

3

4

5

6

7

8

9

10

11

12

13

14

15

16

1 Mix egg yolks, sugar, flour, and vanilla in the saucepan.

2 Add milk and cook gently, stirring all the time until the mixture thickens into a custard.

3 Pour the custard into the cake pan and let it cool. Chill in the refrigerator until firm.

4 Cut the custard into squares and coat each square with beaten egg and breadcrumbs. Ask an adult to heat the butter in a frying pan and fry each square until it is browned. Use the sieve to sprinkle powdered sugar over each square. Serve this treat hot.

GLOSSARY

capuchones, 15	Hoods worn by *nazarenos*.
costaleros, 14	Men who carry floats during Holy Week processions.
diverse, 4	Of wide variety and great range.
effigies, 11	Images or physical representations of people or objects.
fallas, 9	Huge floats burned on Saint Joseph's Day.
flamenco, 3, 19	A type of dance with strong rhythms and beautiful costumes.
Gypsies, 26	An ethnic group in Spain.
makeshift, 17	Temporary.
matadors, 23	Bullfighters.
nazarenos, 15	People who carry big, heavy crosses in Holy Week processions.
palos, 27	Styles of flamenco.
rivalry, 11	Competition between groups fighting for the same prize.
spectacular, 8	Captivating and amazing.
sponsored, 6	Paid for the cost of a project on someone else's behalf.
vagabonds, 26	People who move from place to place with no permanent home.

INDEX

Picture credits
BES Stock: 2; Camera Press: 15 (bottom), 21 (bottom), 24, 25 (bottom); DDB Stock Photo: 5, 21 (top); Haga Library: 1, 7, 8, 9 (top), 10, 12, 14 (bottom), 18 (top), 22 (bottom), 27; HBL Network: 13 (top), 19 (bottom), 26; Ingrid Horstmann: 14 (top), 15 (top); David Simson: 3 (top), 4, 6 (left), 9 (bottom), 11, 20 (both), 22 (top), 23; Liba Taylor: 13 (bottom); Topham Picturepoint: 16, 17, 19 (top), 25 (top); Trip Photographic Library: 3 (bottom), 6 (right), 18 (bottom), 28

Digital scanning by Superskill Graphics Pte Ltd